JAVA PROGRAMMING 1
STUDY GUIDE

SERGIO PISANO, Ed.D.

Warning and Disclaimer:

Every effort has been made to make this booklet as complete and as accurate as possible. The author, publisher, and their agents assume no responsibility for errors or omissions. Nor do they assume liability or responsibility to any person or entity with respect to any loss or damages arising from the use of information contained therein.

ISBN-13: 978-0-578-96135-4

Cover Design: Sergio Pisano.

HOW TO USE THIS GUIDE

The goal of this booklet is to provide a condensed study guide of the most important and basic concepts covered in first level Java programming courses using a cram sheet format with the least possible number of pages for convenience and effectiveness. It is not meant to be a comprehensive source or substitute for formal textbooks or any other learning resource. Therefore, it is recommended to use this guide only after reviewing formal learning materials or in conjunction with them, as a quick summarized overview of important Java programming concepts. It can also be used as a quick refresher for anyone returning to programming in Java and needing to get up to speed quickly.

This booklet's content follows the curriculum commonly used in first level college Java programming courses leaving behind concepts that are normally covered at higher levels. While this guide provides a good theoretical summary of Java programming concepts and syntax with some basic examples, it is crucial for students to remember that programming is a skill that needs to be put into practice. It requires dedication, time, lots of trial-and-error, and patience. This study guide provides one more tool in the students' arsenal to help them succeed.

Basic Terms

Java Executing Process: Java is both a compiled and interpreted language; Source code contained in .java files is compiled into "byte code" producing .class files, then it is interpreted by the Java Virtual Machine.

Java Virtual Machine (JVM): Interpreter for Java compiled files (.class) on a specific computer.

Java Runtime Environment (JRE): Software package containing libraries, the JVM, and other components to run Java applications.

Java Development Kit (JDK): Java compiler that produces .class files and includes the JRE.

Java Standard Edition (JSE): Used to develop client-side standalone applications.

Java Enterprise Edition (JEE): Used to develop server-side applications.

Java Micro Edition (JME): Used to develop mobile applications.

Basic Flow Chart Symbols

Symbol	Name	Meaning
→	Flowline (arrow)	Used to connect symbols and indicate the flow of logic.
(oval)	Terminal (oval)	Used to represent the beginning (Start) or the end (End) of a task.
(parallelogram)	Input/Output (Parallelogram)	Used for input and output operations, such as reading and displaying. Data to be read or displayed are described inside.
(rectangle)	Processing (rectangle)	Used for arithmetic and data-manipulation operations. The instructions are listed inside the symbol.
(diamond)	Decision (diamond)	Used for any logic or comparison operations. Has one entry and two exit paths (yes/no).
(circle)	Connector (circle)	Used to connect lines.
- - - [Comment	Comment	Used to add comments to the chart.

Problem Solving Methodology: Process of defining a problem, searching and finding all relevant information about it, and discovering, designing, and evaluating solutions.

Computing Problems: Special type of problems generally involving inputs, processing (actions), and outputting of solutions or results.

Divide-and-Conquer Method: Common problem solving method that takes a larger problem and brakes it into smaller ones that are worked on and resolved one-by-one independently.

Hierarchy (Structure) Chart: Common first step in solution design that provides a high level view of broken down components (or tasks) of a bigger problem (program). These charts do not contain any pseudocode, are read top-to-bottom and left-to-right.

Flow Chart: Graphical depiction of the logical steps needed to carry out a task showing how each step relates to each other. They are part of a divide-and-conquer method to approach problems.

Pseudocode: Informal way to write a program using English-like phrases to outline a task.

Source Code: Computer code used to create a program in a specific programming language. In Java, source code is stored in .java files.

Machine Code: Translated (compiled) source code into instructions (low-level code) that computers can understand and execute.

Compilation: Single-step process (all at once) of converting an entire source code from a program into executable (low-level) machine code for a specific computer architecture to execute. In Java, compiled code is stored in .class files.

Interpreter: Intermediary application that converts and executes source code into machine code one statement at a time allowing it to execute in any architecture that has an interpreter.

Integrated Development Environment (IDE): Software that provides tools to facilitate the creation of source code in a specific programming language (e.g., Eclipse, NetBeans, BlueJ, etc.).

Command Line Interface (CLI): Non-graphical interface to execute commands and programs in a computer.

Questions:

Notes: . . . .
. . . .
. . . .
. . . .
. . . .
. . . .
. . . .
. . . .
. . . .
. . . .
. . . .
. . . .
. . . .
. . . .
. . . .
. . . .
. . . .
. . . .
. . . .
. . . .
. . . .
. . . .
. . . .
. . . .
. . . .
. . . .
. . . .
. . . .
. . . .
. . . .
. . . .
. . . .
. . . .
. . . .
. . . .
. . . .
. . . .

Summary:

Java Basics

Primitive Types: Basic types of stored primitive data (byte, short, int, long, float, double, boolean, char).

Reference Types: Any instantiable class, array, & interface that stores memory addresses (e.g., String, Scanner, String [], etc.)

Java Primitive Types

Data Type	Contains	Range of values
byte	An integer.	-128 to +127.
short	An integer.	-32768 to +32767.
int	An integer.	-2147483648 to +2147483647.
long	An integer.	-9223372036854775808 to +9223372036854775807.
float	Real number.	-3.40282347E+38 to +3.40282347E+38.
double	Real number.	-1.79769...E+308 to +1.79769...E+308.
char	A character.	A - Z, a - z, 0 - 9, !@#$%^&*() etc. Denote literals in single quotes (e.g., 'c').
boolean	A boolean value.	Only two possible values: true and false.

Java Operators Evaluation Precedence Order

Order	Operator	Description	Associativity
1st	[] . ()	Access array element. Access object member. Parentheses.	Left to right.
2nd	++ --	Unary post-increment. Unary post-decrement.	Not associative.
3rd	++ -- + - ! ~	Unary pre-increment. Unary pre-decrement. Unary plus. Unary minus. Unary logical NOT. Unary bitwise NOT.	Right to left.
4th	() new	Cast. Object creation.	Right to left.
5th	* / %	Multiplicative.	Left to right.
6th	+ - +	Additive. String concatenation.	Left to right.
7th	<< >> >>>	Shift.	Left to right.
8th	< <= > >= instanceof	Relational.	Not associative.
9th	== !=	Equality.	Left to right.
10th	&	Bitwise AND.	Left to right.
11th	^	Bitwise XOR.	Left to right.
12th	|	Bitwise OR.	Left to right.
13th	&&	Logical AND.	Left to right.
14th	||	Logical OR.	Left to right.
15th	?:	Ternary.	Right to left.
16th	= += -= *= /= %= &= ^= |= <<= >>= >>>=	Assignment.	Right to left.

String Literal: A sequence of characters to be printed.

Escape Sequence: A special sequence of characters used to insert special characters in a string.

\t tab character   \n new line character

\" quotation mark character   \\ backslash character

Comments: Notes written in source code by the programmer to describe or clarify the code. It is good practice to always include comments at the top of each source code file (comment header), and at the start of every class, method, and complex code block explaining it.

// Single Line Comment   /* Multi-line Comment */

Variable (field): Named container for storing data values.

Expression: Series of variables, operators, and method calls that evaluates to a single value (e.g., 1 +1).

Statement: Complete execution unit (e.g., System.*out*.println ("Test");).

Assignment (=): Copies the content of right hand side into left hand side variable (e.g., x = 1). For primitives, value is copied. For references, address is copied (objects are shared).

Declaration: Process of defining a variable (or method) for the first time.

Comparisons (==): Compares the content of variables. For references, the addresses are compared.

Relational Operators: <, >, <=, >=, ==, !=

Block: Grouped statements within curvy brackets.

System.*out*.println: Prints a line of output on console (.print does not move cursor to a new line).

```java
public class Driver {
  public static void main(String[] args)
  {
    int myVariable = 5; //declares-initialize variable
    System.out.println("Hello user number:" + myVariable);
  }
}
```

Questions:

Notes: . . . .
. . . .
. . . .
. . . .
. . . .
. . . .
. . . .
. . . .
. . . .
. . . .
. . . .
. . . .
. . . .
. . . .
. . . .
. . . .
. . . .
. . . .
. . . .
. . . .
. . . .
. . . .
. . . .
. . . .
. . . .
. . . .
. . . .
. . . .
. . . .
. . . .
. . . .
. . . .
. . . .
. . . .

Summary:

Java Object-Oriented Programming Basics

Object Oriented Programming (OOP): Methodology based on the concept of "objects" instead of procedures.

Class: Container serving as a blueprint to hold code (e.g., "Car" class) stored in .java files.

Object: Specific instance of a class (e.g., Mustang, etc.).

Method: Java statements grouped together in a block to serve a specific function in a class (e.g., Accelerate, Brake, etc.). Every Java program starts in the main method. Methods can receive parameters (also called "arguments").

Method Signature: Method's name and parameter list.

Class Syntax

```
/* Description of the class */
accessSpecifier class ClassName
{
    accessSpecifier fieldType fieldName; // Description of field        Fields Section

    // Description of Constructor Purpose                               Constructors Section
    accessSpecifier ClassName(paramType paramName, paramType paramName)
    {
        // Constructor Body
    }

    // Description of method purpose                                    Methods Section
    accessSpecifier returnType methodName(paramType paramName, paramType paramName)
    {
        // Method body
    }
}
```

```java
// Example of a Car class
public class Car {
    private int miles; // car's miles
    private String owner; // car's owner
    //Constructor: Initializes car
    public Car() {
        miles= 0;
        owner="Dealer"; }
    //Getter: gets car's miles
    public int getMiles() {
        return miles; }
    //Getter: gets car owner name
    public String getOwner() {
        return owner; }
    //Setter: sets car's miles
    public void setMiles (int myMiles) {
        miles = myMiles; }
    //Setter: sets car's miles
    public void setOwner (String newOwner) {
        owner = newOwner;
    }
}
```

Encapsulation: One of the tenets of object-oriented programming that aims to hide sensitive data of a class from users (using the private access modifier) and group related data and behaviors into a single unit.

Constructors: Special method called when an object is instantiated to initialize object before its use. Constructor's name must match name of class, have no return type, may not return any values, and are typically public. If a constructor is not defined, Java provides a default constructor (with no parameters).

Getters (Accessors) Methods: Class methods written by programmer to extract/access privately declared data.

Setters (Mutators) Methods: Class methods written by programmer to store data in class.

Creating an Object of a Class (Instantiation):

Accessing (Calling) Class Methods and Members:

Syntax: object.method(parameters)

Example: myMustang.accelerate();

Syntax: object.membervariable

Method Overloading: Creating a class method with the same name as an existing one but with different parameters.

"this" Keyword: used to reference a member of the current object (e.g., this.miles=500;)

Questions:

Notes: ....
....
....
....
....
....
....
....
....
....
....
....
....
....
....
....
....
....
....
....
....
....
....
....
....
....
....
....
....
....
....
....
....
....
....
....
....
....
....
....

Summary:

Object-Oriented Programming Quick Summary

- Object Oriented Programming (OOP) is a programming methodology based on the concept of "classes" and "objects". A class is like a blueprint that contains code. When planning a program based on a problem statement and requirements, first identify the classes need. Candidates for classes will normally be nouns. For example, in a school's program, Student, Teacher, and Course could be candidates for classes. Once identified, eliminate duplicates and out of scope candidate classes. Next, identify each class fields. Fields are variables containing data that describe an object of a class. For example, a Social Security Number, name, and address identify a Student. Finally, identify actions the class needs to perform. These actions will be the class methods. For example, a Student can register or drop courses, etc. Methods will normally be named after verbs. Once classes, methods, and fields are identified, present them in an UML Class Diagram to help visualize and organize the program's plan.

- Similar to a factory where blueprints are needed to produce items, in OOP produced items are called "objects" and are created ("instantiated") based on a class (blueprint). An object is also referred to as an "instance" of a class since there can be many "instances" of it at any given time (e.g., you can have 60 objects of the Student Class representing specific students).

- Each class must deal with its own specific methods and fields. Data not belonging to a specific class should not be included in it (e.g., identifying data from teachers should not be stored in the Student class). This practice is called "abstraction" and it aims to hide complexity from users showing them only relevant information. This also allows for another tenet of object-oriented programming: encapsulation. Encapsulation protects data stored in a class from system-wide access so that programmers retain control of it and avoid security holes.

- Encapsulation and abstraction are extremely important tenets of OOP for many reasons, including the need to organize and store relevant data, code reusability (as we want to be able to reuse classes in different programs with little or no changes to them), and security and control (as we want to keep control of what a class contains and how it can be used). All these factors make things much easier for users and programmers. For example, when using the Scanner class to receive input from the console, a class that somebody else created, we do not have to know what code it contains, only its purpose and how to invoke its methods (nextInt, nextLine, etc.).

- Methods contain code that perform specific actions for a class and can accept variables as "parameters" allowing data to move from one place to another in the code flow and overcome scope limitations.

- To use a class, we need to create objects of it. Each .java file normally contains a class. The "Driver" class normally contains the "main" method (starting point of the entire program). The main method is where the compiler expects to find its first instructions and is where objects are commonly instantiated to coordinate/manipulate their high-level functions.

- Each class also has a special public method called "constructor". When an object of a class is created, the instructions inside its constructor method will execute first (thus the name "constructor"). A constructor is the starting point of the object's life, similarly to how the "main" method in the Driver class is the starting point of the entire Java program. Inside the constructor is where we will normally initialize an object's fields. Depending on where we declare a variable in a class, it will have different scopes (or range of availability). Instance fields are always declared at the start of the class and outside any method. Therefore, their scope will be the entire class (in other words, any element in the class can access them).

- Similar classes can be grouped in a "package". If a class from a specific class is needed , it will need to be imported first.

- Access of a class and its members is determined by their access specifier. If no access specifier is defined, the default will allow access of an element within the class and package, but not from outside the package. A public access specifier will allow access everywhere, while a private access specifier will grant access of an element only within the class. A protected access specifier will allow access within the package and outside of it only through a child class.

- Classes also have "setter" and "getter" methods. They are in charge of either setting private field's value of an object or retrieving them for usage. Although we can do this directly in our program (if fields are declared as public), this should be avoided because it creates security holes in your class and breaks encapsulation (designer of the class would lose control of who can change the fields of your object and how).

Questions:

Notes: ....
....
....
....
....
....
....
....
....
....
....
....
....
....
....
....
....
....
....
....
....
....
....
....
....
....
....
....
....
....
....
....
....
....
....
....

Summary:

Java Basics

Parts of a Method's Declaration:

```
  modifier  return-type  method-name        parameter

  public double accelerate(int myValue)
  {
      double accelerationFactor = (10 + myValue);
      return accelerationFactor;
  }
```

Passing Parameters: Parameters in methods are treated as local variables within the method. They are passed "by value" (copy). If the parameter is referencing an object, it is the reference that is passed to the method. Local variables and parameters are deleted when the method finishes execution.

Formal Parameter: Parameter value that is listed in the method's declaration.

Actual Parameter: Parameter that is given when method is called.

Returning Values: Data returned by a method to where it was called.

Method Overloading: Definition of new method with the same name of another already existing, but with different parameters.

Java Package: Group of similar types of classes, interfaces, and sub-packages. The package keyword is used to create a package in Java. Statement is placed at start of a class (e.g., package mypackage;).

Scope: Refers to the part of a program that has access to a specific program resource.

Shadowing: When a method has a local variable with the same name as an instance field (not recommended).

Java Access Specifier: Placed on declaration of instance variables (fields) and methods to define access scope.

Java Access Specifiers

Access Specifier	Within Class	Within Package	Subclass Within Package Only	Global
Private	Y	N	N	N
Default	Y	Y	N	N
Protected	Y	Y	Y	N
Public	Y	Y	Y	Y

Local Variable: Variable declared inside a method. Its scope begins at the declaration of the variable and ends at the end of the method (or block) in which it was declared.

Instance Variable (field): Variable declared inside a class but outside all methods. Its scope is the entire class.

Class (Static) Variable: Variable declared with the static keyword in a class. Only one copy of a static variable exists per class that is shared among all of its objects. Scope is the entire class.

```
public class Car {
    int horsePower; //Public Instance Variable
    private double carCost; // Private Instance Variable
    static int makerYear; //Static Variable
    public double accelerate() {
        double accelerationFactor = 10.5; //Local Variable
        return (accelerationFactor+5);
    }
}
```

Java Naming Conventions

Classes: Capitalize every first letter of each word (e.g., UpperCamelCase). Classes should be nouns.

Variables and Methods: Make first word lowercase and capitalize first letter of each subsequent word, this is called camel notation (e.g. areaCounter). Methods should be verbs.

Constants: Declared using **final**. Capitalize every letter and use underscores between words (e.g., **final int** MAX_VALUE = 10;)

Package: All lowercase. Formally, it should start with reverse Internet domain name of company (e.g., com.acme.mypackage).

Object's State: Current value of object's instance variables.

toString Method: Method created by every class automatically to display the state of an object (can be overridden by the programmer).

System.*out*.printf: prints formatted output on the console.

```
double grossPay = 123.12;
System.out.printf("Your pay is %8.2f\n", grossPay);
```

Prints: Your pay is   123.12

%: Placeholder for variable.   **8:** Output field width.
.2: Two decimal points.   **\n:** new line escape sequence.
 f: float number (e.g., d for decimal, i for integer, etc.).

Questions:

Notes: ....
....
....
....
....
....
....
....
....
....
....
....
....
....
....
....
....
....
....
....
....
....
....
....
....
....
....
....
....
....
....
....
....

Summary:

Java Basics

Import: Packages-libraries-classes can be imported into Java source code using the import statement at the start of the code. Syntax: **import** packagename.className; or to import all classes in the package: **import** packagename.*;

Prompt: A message telling the user what input to type.

Token: A token is a series of characters that ends with what Java calls whitespace. A whitespace character can be a blank, a tab character, a carriage return, or the end of a file.

Scanner Class: Used to get input from user in the console. Must be imported and then instantiated to use its methods depending on the data type we want our input to take.

Some Scanner Class Methods

Method	Description
nextInt()	Reads a token of user input as an int.
nextDouble()	Reads a token of user input as a double.
next()	Reads a token of user input as a String.
nextLine()	Reads a line of user input as a String.

```
import java.util.Scanner;
public class Car {
  public static void main(String[] args) {
    int carMiles;
    Scanner in = new Scanner(System.in); //Instantiation
    System.out.print("Enter Odometer: ");
    carMiles = in.nextInt(); //Scanner nextInt method
    System.out.println("You entered: " + carMiles + " Miles");
  }
}
```

Comparing Floating Point Values: == and != may not work as expected for floating point values due to precision limitations and discrepancies among computers. One way to address this is by testing a range of values. We might define some small value, say EPSILON, and compare to see if the two values are within an EPSILON of each other. We consider the values equal if they are within the EPSILON.

```
double x = 1 - 0.1 - 0.1 - 0.1 - 0.1 - 0.1;
final double EPSILON = 0.000001; //Defined precision
if(Math.abs(x - 0.5) < EPSILON) {
System.out.println("They are equal");
}
```

Java Default Data Type: When writing a floating point literal, Java assumes it is a double by default.

Coercion: Automatic conversion of a data type to another widening the value (e.g., **double** x = 0; //x becomes a double: 0.0).

Math Class: Does not need to be imported or instantiated. Contains methods to perform common mathematical operations.

Some Math Class Methods

Method	Returns
Math.sqrt(x)	Returns square root of x.
Math.pow(x,y)	Returns x raised to power of y.
Math.sin(x)	Returns sine of x.
Math.cos(x)	Returns cosine of angle x.
Math.tan(x)	Returns tangent of angle x.
Math.asin(x)	Returns arc sine of the specified argument.
Math.acos(x)	Returns arc cosine of x.
Math.atan(x)	Returns inverse tangent function of a value.
Math.exp(x)	Returns Euler's number e raised to the power of x.
Math.log(x)	Returns natural logarithm of x.
Math.log10(x)	Returns base 10 logarithm of specified value.
Math.round(x)	Returns closest integer to x as a long.
Math.abs(x)	Returns absolute value of x.
Math.max(x,y)	Returns maximum of two values x and y.
Math.min(x,y)	Returns minimum of two values x and y.
Math.PI	Returns 3.14159265358979323846 as double.
Math.E	Returns 2.7182818284590452354 as double.

Generating Random Numbers: Done by either using Math.random that generates a double >= 0.0 and < 1.0 (e.g., **int** value = (int)(Math.random() * 10) + 1;//Returns 1 to 10), or using the Random class (needs to be imported) and its methods (e.g., .nextInt).

```
import java.util.Random;
public class RandomExample
{
  public static void main(String[] args) {
    Random g = new Random();
    int value = g.nextInt(10) + 1; //int between 1 to 10
  }
}
```

Questions:

Notes: . . . .
. . . .
. . . .
. . . .
. . . .
. . . .
. . . .
. . . .
. . . .
. . . .
. . . .
. . . .
. . . .
. . . .
. . . .
. . . .
. . . .
. . . .
. . . .
. . . .
. . . .
. . . .
. . . .
. . . .
. . . .
. . . .
. . . .
. . . .
. . . .
. . . .
. . . .
. . . .
. . . .
. . . .
. . . .

Summary:

Java Basics

UML (Unified Modeling Language) Class Diagrams: Graphical representation of classes using language for modeling the structure and behavior of object-oriented systems widely used in industry to design, develop and document software.

UML Class Associations (Relationships): Represented by a line connecting UML class boxes. There are several types. The most basic-common is the "Uses-as" association implemented by creating methods that return or use variables from the related class. If a particular relationship only works in one direction, we use an open arrow to specialize it.

Multiplicity: Given an association between two objects, A and B, we state how many 'A's are associated with 'B's (min, max).

UML Class Diagram

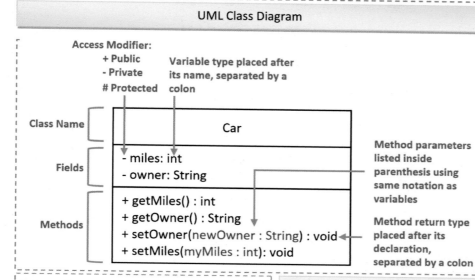

Access Modifier:
+ Public
- Private
Protected

Variable type placed after its name, separated by a colon

Class Name

Car

Fields
- miles: int
- owner: String

Methods
+ getMiles() : int
+ getOwner() : String
+ setOwner(newOwner : String) : void
+ setMiles(myMiles : int): void

Method parameters listed inside parenthesis using same notation as variables

Method return type placed after its declaration, separated by a colon

How to Approach an OOP Task:

1. Identify all of the nouns and nouns phrases.
2. Combine or remove redundant-repeated nouns.
3. Remove out of scope nouns.
4. Remove program constructs.
5. Identify and remove attributes from the list.
6. Identify relationships and each class responsibilities and create UML diagram.

String Class: In Java, strings are stored in objects of the String class using a special way. This has many benefits, including memory efficiency and many methods to manipulate strings. When creating a String object, It is recommended not to use the **new** keyword and use string literal instantiation instead (e.g., String myText = "Hello there";). Using this method, the JVM checks a pool filled with strings constants for the existence of a string we want to store. If it exists, a reference to the pooled instance is returned. If not, a new string instance is created and placed in the pool.

Static Methods: Methods shared among all instances of its class objects without the need of instantiation. Useful for utilitarian purposes and similar to procedural functions. Can only access static data and call other static methods. It cannot be overridden, refer to "this" or "super" keywords.

Frequently Used String Methods

Method	Description
str1.equals(str2)	Returns Boolean.
str1.equalsIgnoreCase(str2)	Returns Boolean.
str1.compareTo(str2)	Returns an int: positive if str1 > str2, 0 if equal, negative if str1 < str2.
str1.length( )	Returns the number of characters stored in str1.
str1.concat(str2)	Concatenation, same as str1 + str2.
str1.charAt(i)	Returns the character at index i of str1.
str1.replace(char1, char2)	Returns a version of str1 where every instance of character char1 is replaced by char2.
str1.trim( )	Return a version of str1 with no leading and trailing white space.

```
String myString = "Hello World";
System.out.println(myString.replace('o', '@')); //Returns "Hell@ W@rld"
```

```
public static double milesToKilometers(double miles) { return miles * 1.609; }
public static void main(String[] args) { System.out.println(milesToKilometers(30.5));} //Calls Static Method
```

Questions:

Notes: . . . .
. . . .
. . . .
. . . .
. . . .
. . . .
. . . .
. . . .
. . . .
. . . .
. . . .
. . . .
. . . .
. . . .
. . . .
. . . .
. . . .
. . . .
. . . .
. . . .
. . . .
. . . .
. . . .
. . . .
. . . .
. . . .
. . . .
. . . .
. . . .
. . . .
. . . .
. . . .
. . . .
. . . .
. . . .
. . . .
. . . .

Summary:

Java Selections and Loops Basics

If Statement Syntax:
```
if ( boolean expression )
        { statement(s); }
Else
        { statement(s); }
```

```
if (age>18) {
        System.out.println("Can vote"); }
else {
        System.out.println("Can not vote"); }
```

Switch Statement Syntax:
```
switch(variable) {
        case value_1:  statement(s); break;
        case value_2:  statement(s); break;
        ...
        case value_n:  statement(s); break;
        default: statement(s); }
```

```
String letter=""; double gpa=0;
switch (letter) {
        case "A":  gpa = 4.0; break;
        case "B":  gpa = 3.0; break;
        case "C":  gpa = 2.0; break;
        case "D":  gpa = 1.0; break;
        case "F":  gpa = 0.0; }
```

for Statement: Pre-test loop used where there is some type of counting variable that can be evaluated.
for Statement Syntax:
```
for ( initialization ; boolean expression ; increment )
        { statement(s); }
```

```
int y=0;
for (int x = 2; x <= 4; x++) {
        y = y + x;
        System.out.println("Value of x:" + x);
}
```

break Statement: Exists execution of a loop.
continue Statement: Skips rest of loop body. Control returns back at the condition of loop.
Nested Loops: Loop inside another loop.
Sentinel (Flag) Value: Special value in the context of a computer program used as a condition of termination, typically in a loop or recursive algorithm.
Infinite Loop: Loop that never ends or exits.

Conditional Operator Syntax:
```
(condition) ? returnTrueValue : ReturnFalseValue;
(e.g., z = (x > y) ? 0 : 1;)
```

Java Logical Operators

Operator	Description	Java Symbol
AND	All individual conditions must be true for the AND to be true.	&&
OR	At least one individual condition must be true for the OR to be true.	||
NOT	Negates or reverses a Boolean value.	!
XOR	XOR is true if one of the two individual conditions is true and the other is false.	^

while Loop: Pre-test loop that executes statements if condition is false at the beginning.
while Statement Syntax:
```
while ( boolean expression )
        { statement(s); }
```

```
int x=1; int y=0;
while (x < 1000000) {
        x = x * 2;
        y = x;
}
```

do-while Statement: Post-test loop that executes statements at least once.
do-while Statement Syntax:
```
do {
    statement(s);
    } while (boolean expression );
```

```
Scanner in = new Scanner(System.in);
int sum = 0, value;
do
{
        System.out.print("Enter a number (0 to exit): ");
        value = in.nextInt();
        if (value!=0) sum+=value;
} while (value!=0);
System.out.println("The sum is " + sum);
```

Questions:

Notes: . . . .
. . . .
. . . .
. . . .
. . . .
. . . .
. . . .
. . . .
. . . .
. . . .
. . . .
. . . .
. . . .
. . . .
. . . .
. . . .
. . . .
. . . .
. . . .
. . . .
. . . .
. . . .
. . . .
. . . .
. . . .
. . . .
. . . .
. . . .
. . . .
. . . .
. . . .
. . . .
. . . .
. . . .
. . . .
. . . .
. . . .

Summary:

Java Arrays Basics

Array: Object that stores a collection of indexed values (or other objects) of same type.

Syntax	Example
Array Declaration: type[] name = new type[size];	int[] numbers = **new int**[6];
Accessing Array's Element: name [Index]	numbers[0] = 20;
Array Initialization: type[] name = {value1,..., valueN};	String[]weekEndDays = {"Sunday", Saturday"};

String Arrays: Each element of a String array is a String object, therefore, String methods of a specific String object inside the array may be called using the array's name and index number. For example: System.*out*.println(weekEndDays [0].toUpperCase());)

```
//Filling & Accessing an Array Using for Loops
int[] myArray = new int[5];
    //Filling Array
    for (int i=0; i<5; i++) {
        myArray[i]=1; }
    //Accessing Array
    for (int i=0; i<5; i++) {
        System.out.print(myArray[i] + " "); }
```

Enhanced for Loop: Simplified for loop used with arrays.
Enhanced for Loop Syntax:
for (datatype elementVariable : array)
    { statement(s) };

```
int[] numbers = {1, 3, 5, 7};
for (int myValue: numbers) {
    System.out.println(myValue); }
```

Array Searching Algorithms: Ways to search a value in an array, including: Sequential Search (slowest), Binary Search (array needs to be sorted), Selection Sort, etc.
Arrays Class: Provides specialized methods to manipulate arrays (needs: import java.util.Arrays;)

```
int[] numbers = {4, 2, 1, 3};
Arrays.sort(numbers); //Sorts Array

//Shows Array Elements:
System.out.println(Arrays.toString(numbers));
int searchValue=1; //Value to Search in Array

//Seeks Value Using Binary Search Method:
System.out.println("\n" + searchValue + " found at: "
+ Arrays.binarySearch(numbers,searchValue) +
" index");
```

Array Element Index Number: Index number assigned to a location inside an array starting from 0.
Array length Field: Field of an array object that stores size of array starting from 1 (e.g., System.*out*.println(weekEndDays.length);)
Array Shallow Copying: Copying the reference of an array only (e.g., **int**[] array2 = array1;).
Array Deep Copying: Copying each individual element of one array to another. This is done using a for loop or specialized method.
Two-Dimensional Array: Array of arrays using two sets of brackets holding indexes (first represents row, and second column).
Ragged Array: Array of arrays where the number of columns of each row may be different (e.g., **int** [][] triangleArray = **new int** [5][];)

```
int[][] numbers = { {1, 2, 3}, {4, 5, 6}, {7, 8, 9} }; // 3x3 Array Declaration
System.out.println("Value of Row 2 Column 1 in numbers Array: " +
numbers[2][1]); //Accessing numbers Array (Index starts from 0)
double[][] scores = new double[3][4]; // 3 Rows x 4 Columns Array
Scanner keyboardInput = new Scanner(System.in);
for (int row = 0; row < 3; row++) { //Filling scores Array
        for (int col = 0; col < 4; col++) {
                System.out.print("Enter a score:");
                scores[row][col] = keyboardInput.nextDouble(); } }
```

ArrayList Class: ArrayList also allows object storage but automatically expands or shrinks. Needs: **import** java.util.ArrayList; and uses the Collections class for searches.

```
// Create an ArrayList of names (String objects).
ArrayList<String> nameList = new ArrayList<String>();
nameList.add("Mei");
nameList.add("Sergio");
nameList.remove(1); //Removes Sergio
for (String myName : nameList) { // Display Items in the ArrayList.
        System.out.println(myName);
}
```

Questions:

Notes: . . . .
. . . .
. . . .
. . . .
. . . .
. . . .
. . . .
. . . .
. . . .
. . . .
. . . .
. . . .
. . . .
. . . .
. . . .
. . . .
. . . .
. . . .
. . . .
. . . .
. . . .
. . . .
. . . .
. . . .
. . . .
. . . .
. . . .
. . . .
. . . .
. . . .
. . . .
. . . .
. . . .

Summary:

Java Basics

Boxing: Placing a primitive type value in a wrapper class.

Unboxing: Taking a primitive type value out of a wrapper class.

```java
int myInt=0;
Integer myIntObject = new Integer(myInt); //Boxing (Wrapping)
Integer myIntObject2 = (myInt); // Auto-Boxing

int myUnBoxedInt = myIntObject.intValue(); //unBoxing
int myUnBoxedInt2 = myIntObject2; // Auto-unBoxing
```

Wrapper Class toString Method: Each of the numeric wrapper classes has a static toString method that converts its number (argument) and returns a string representation of that number.

```java
double d = 10.95;
String str1 = Double.toString(d); //Converts double to String
```

Wrapper Classes: Classes that "wrap" primitive type values into objects in order to use methods and OOP properties.

Primitive	Wrapper Class	Constructor Argument
boolean	Boolean	boolean or String.
byte	Byte	byte or String.
char	Character	char.
int	Integer	int or String.
float	Float	float, double, or String.
double	Double	double or String.
long	Long	long or String.
short	Short	short or String.

Wrapper Class MIN_VALUE and MAX_VALUE: Static final variables of numeric wrapper classes holding the minimum and maximum values for a particular data type.

Writing & Reading Text Files: Java provides many ways to read and write text files including the classes: File, FileWritter, PrintWritter, etc.

File Location Note: When defining the path of a text file in code, if a backslash is used in a string literal and not in a String object, it must be escaped as shown in this example:
PrintWriter outFile = **new** PrintWriter ("C:\\myFileName.txt");

Parse Method: Converts string representation of a number to its numeric equivalent.

Java Parse Methods

Method	Usage	Example Code
Byte.parseByte	Converts a string to a byte.	byte num; num = Byte.parseByte(str);
Double.parseDouble	Converts a string to a double.	double num; num = Double.parseDouble(str);
Float.parseFloat	Converts a string to a float.	float num; num = Float.parseFloat(str);
Integer.parseInt	Converts a string to an int.	int num; num = Integer.parseInt(str);
Long.parseLong	Converts a string to a long.	long num; num = Long.parseLong(str);
Short.parseShort	Converts a string to a short.	short num; num = Short.parseShort(str);

```java
import java.io.*;  //Appending to a Text File Example
public class FileWriteDemo {
  public static void main(String[] args) throws IOException {
    String fileName="Test.txt."; // File's name
    String myName="Sergio"; // Name to store
    FileWriter fw = new FileWriter(fileName, true); //false to overwrite
    PrintWriter outputFile = new PrintWriter(fw);
    outputFile.println(myName); // Appends name to the file.
    outputFile.close(); // Closes the file.
  }
}
```

```java
//Reading from Text File Example
File file = new File(fileName); // Opens the file.
Scanner inputFile = new Scanner(file);
while ( inputFile.hasNext() ) // Reads from file.
{
     myName = inputFile.nextLine();
     System.out.println(myName);
}
inputFile.close(); // Closes file.
```

Questions:

Notes: . . . .
. . . .
. . . .
. . . .
. . . .
. . . .
. . . .
. . . .
. . . .
. . . .
. . . .
. . . .
. . . .
. . . .
. . . .
. . . .
. . . .
. . . .
. . . .
. . . .
. . . .
. . . .
. . . .
. . . .
. . . .
. . . .
. . . .
. . . .
. . . .
. . . .
. . . .
. . . .
. . . .
. . . .
. . . .

Summary:

REFERENCES & RECOMMENDED SOURCES

1. AP CS A Java Course & AP CSAwesome. (2021). Retrieved from

   https://csawesome.runestone.academy/runestone/books/published/csawesome/index.html

2. Deitel, P. J., & Deitel, H. M. (2018). Java how to program.

3. Gaddis, T. (2018). *Starting out with Java Early objects.*

4. JavaTpoint Tutorials. (2021). Retrieved from https://www.javatpoint.com

5. Sedgewick, R., & Wayne, K. (2017). *Computer science : an interdisciplinary approach.*

6. W3Schools Online Web Tutorials. (2021). Retrieved from https://www.w3schools.com/

7. zyBooks - Interactive Textbooks. (2021). Retrieved from http://www.zybooks.com/home/